Hello, and thank you for choosing to read my book.

My name is Wookie. I am a Yorkshire Terrier, I am seven years old, and I AM th

Yes, that really is me on the front cover.

I have a thing about climbing on logs, fallen trees, even climbing up living trees if I can.

I live in Warwickshire, England, with Hu-Mum, Dog-Dad, three cats, two gerbils and five chickens.

My favourite thing in the world is walkies with Hu-mum and Dog-Dad, especially in the woods. We have lots of adventures.

I first started writing poems when I was just a Pup. Hu-mum recently shared these poems with some of her friends and they all said, 'Wookie should write a book!'. I just thought that sounded like a lot of hard work, but here I am!

The poems in this book are mostly mine, although I have included some written by my friends, and a couple that Hu-mum wrote about me.

I hope you enjoy the poems, and the photographs to illustrate them.

Wookie!

My first poem is a little bit about me, and being a Yorkie.

Yorkies were originally bred to be ratters. They were proper hunting and working dogs.

They worked in factories and mines, getting rid of vermin, and poachers loved them because they were small enough to put into a pocket to hide from Gamekeepers. They were also incredibly brave, standing up to creatures much bigger than they were.

A bit like me with that sheep in Wales! I'll tell you more about that later!

Of course, nowadays most people think of Yorkies as lap dogs. I don't mind a little bit of sitting on Hu-Mums lap, but I'm still an 1800's Yorkie at heart. I'm happiest out in the woods, tracking smells, scaring rabbits and squirrels, and sometimes even chasing a deer.

I have despatched rats, too. They come into the garden to try to steal food put out for the chickens. I'm not standing for that!

Dog-Dad saw me get one once, and was all 'Eew. No. That's nasty. Yuk!'

Hu-Mum just called me a 'Good Girl' and got a poo bag to put the rat in!

BEING A YORKIE

Now I'm a Yorkshire Terrier
I'm loyal, brave and smart,
I may be small in stature,
But I am huge in heart.

My heritage is noble,
We had a job to do,
We kept homes free of vermin,
And worked in factories too.

Genetics still compel me,
I have to hunt my prey,
Rabbits, squirrels, all fair game,
If they should come my way.

Once I'm out there in the woods,
I truly know no fear,
I'm not afraid of anything,
I'll even chase the deer.

But one thing I don't understand
And neither do the cats,
Though Hu-Mums made it VERY clear,
Gerbils ARE NOT rats!

My next poem is called 'Keep Rolling' and it's about something ALL dogs like to do!

Roll in smelly stuff.

I don't understand why humans get so upset.

It's a survival thing, honestly!

We roll in smelly stuff to hide our scent from predators, like lions, and tigers, and bears, oh my!

Okay, so we don't really HAVE any of those in Great Britain…. except for in zoos and stuff, but YOU NEVER KNOW!

Be prepared!

KEEP ROLLING

I like to roll in smelly stuff,

It's just what us dogs do,

Dead things are quite stinky,

But best of all is poo.

Great big sloppy cow pats,

Just tempt me to dive in,

If something feels so awesome,

How can it be a sin?

The USA has skunk stink,

I bet that really rocks,

But for us dogs in Britain,

Our perfume's 'eau de fox'.

We'll smell it from a distance,

And off flat out we'll go,

Our humans left behind us,

Shouting 'No, no, no, no, NO!'

We reach it and start rolling,

It's on our ears and nose,

It's caked on back and tummy,

And squished between our toes.

It really is quite fragrant,

It makes our humans gag,

Especially when it's on our tail,

And launched with every wag.

We're proud of our aroma,

But humans get last laugh

As soon as we get home again,

They throw us in the bath!

STILL WORTH IT!

This next poem is about something silly I did when I was very young.

I didn't always listen to Hu-Mum and Dog-Dad back then, I was still learning that when they told me not to do something it was to keep me safe.

I know better now.

You might wonder why Dog-Dad didn't jump in to save me.

I had previous!

Only a month before I was chasing my ball in a stream and went over a drop-off into a pond. Dog-Dad jumped in to save me, even though HE can't swim, only to see me swimming past with my ball.

Hu-Mum was laughing her head off!

JUST BECAUSE IT'S GREEN…..

When I was just a little Pup, I made a big mistake,

It happened on a sunny walk, beside a lovely lake,

I blame the ducks, they tempted me, I tried hard to be good,

But then they quacked, and that was it, I decided that I would!

I ran as fast as I could go, though Dog-Dad shouted 'STOP'

I rushed out onto smooth green grass, and then I felt……the drop!

Then I was swimming for my life, that green stuff WASN'T ground,

I'm sure the ducks were giggling, as I paddled round and round.

I finally got my bearings, and scrambled up the bank,

Pond weed hanging everywhere, and smelling pretty rank.

Dog-Dad had no sympathy, all he could do was laugh,

I thought that he was pretty mean. That was a SCARY bath.

And so, I learned a rule that day, which onto you I'll pass,

Don't think that just because it's green, that it is ALWAYS grass!

This next poem is also about water, although I didn't fall in this time.

I could have though!

It wasn't really Dog-Dads fault. He was trying to do something nice for Hu-Mum and me.

Here in the UK we have lots of canals, which were built to transport goods before we had lorries, and trains, and aeroplanes.

Now people spend holidays on then, on Canal Boats, sometimes called narrow boats or barges.

Some people live on them.

I wouldn't want to live on one, unless it NEVER MOVED!

IT'S KNOT FOR ME

I have such lovely humans, they really are the best

But now and then they do a 'thing' that puts love to the test.

I'm happy to do most things, I'm up for something new,

But after that experience, there's one thing I won't do.

I really can't blame Dog-Dad, he thought it would be fun

A lovely day out on a boat, relaxing in the sun.

I thought we might go on a cruise, some ocean-going yacht,

But no – it was a narrowboat, a liner it was not.

That said, it started pleasantly, the water gently splashing,

But then the boat went faster, and so began - the crashing.

Apparently, boats do not crash, instead they 'run aground'

Now that's a lie, because I looked. The ground could not be found

I wanted to get off that boat, and just walk on the path

But I was never making it without a nasty bath

So being quite a clever dog, I got myself up high,

So if that boat DID finally sink, I'd be there, safe and dry.

This is the first poem written by someone else.

Hu-Mum wrote it about me.

Hu-Mum doesn't care how filthy I get on walkies, because she knows I've had a great time.

One time, we actually did a 'Mud Run' to raise money for a Dog Rescue.

We both got really muddy.

Hu-Mum even got muddier than me!

I had to have a bath when we got home, but it was worth it.

MUCKY PUP

I look at other Yorkies,

All tidy, clean and neat,

And then I look at Wookie,

Mud – from head to feet,

Her coat is full of thistles,

There's fox poo on her toes,

The only parts not filthy,

Are her eyeballs and her nose,

There's duck weed in her ears,

And twigs caught in her tail,

This is just her normal state,

Each 'walkies' without fail,

She climbs her way through hedges,

She paddles through the crud,

Until it's hard to see what's dog,

And what is simply mud.

But pop her in a soapy bath,

And soon she will scrub up,

I wouldn't change her for the world,

My awesome Mucky Pup.

My next poem isn't just about me…..even though I'm awesome.

It's about dogs in general, and how wonderful we are.

If you have ever been lucky enough to share your life with a dog, you'll know that however much you love them….they love you more.

From the first day you meet, to the day you finally say Goodbye, they will love you.

They want nothing more than to be by your side.

Nothing loves like a dog.

ANGELS WITHOUT WINGS

Some people just like big dogs,

Some people just like small,

Some people just like medium sized,

But most just love them all.

Now some need dogs to guard things,

And some need dogs to herd,

And some need dogs to see for them,

Or hear the spoken word.

Some want to do short walkies,

Some want to take a hike,

Some want an active buddy,

To run beside their bike.

Some want a fancy Pedigree,

Some much prefer a mix,

Some want to cuddle on the couch,

Some want to teach them tricks.

Some want a dog with short fur,

Some want a dog with long,

Some like a dog that's silent,

Some like one with a song,

Some need us as a comfort,

To heal a broken soul,

To save them from their nightmares,

And help their heart feel whole.

It doesn't matter what you need,

What breed, or shape, or size,

Your canine friend will change your life,

Your angel in disguise.

My next poem is about the time Hu-Mum and Dog-Dad decided I needed a friend.

I was worried that they were going to get another dog, and I would have to share all my toys and things, but they didn't.

They got me a kitten!

Yes……a kitten!

They called her Solo, which made them laugh a lot.

Wookie and Solo.

I don't get it!

It's probably something geeky to do with Star Wars.

It gets worse, as you'll find out when you meet the gerbils (ARE NOT RATS!)

I wasn't too keen on Solo to start with, but we're best friends now.

It was fated in the stars!

FLYING SOLO

I can't forget that dreadful day,

The day they got THAT CAT!

A charming, little fluffy ball,

All purry, round and fat,

They thought she would be company,

They thought we'd get on well,

I can't believe how wrong they were,

She is a fiend from Hell!

She lurks up on the cupboard top,

'Til I walk underneath,

Then launches down with six-inch claws,

And Dracula-like teeth.

She hides beneath the sideboard,

To ambush my poor toes,

Then jumps out with a little yowl,

And bites me on my nose

She hangs onto my tail,

She grabs me by the ear,

And though I sometimes tell her off,

She hasn't any fear,

It's said that cats all have nine lives,

But if she doesn't stop,

She'll find out that the number,

Will soon begin to drop!

This poem is about Autumn.

I have to be honest, it's not my favourite season.

It can rain a lot, it can be foggy, and it can be just miserable.

The best thing about it is that I'm an Autumn-coloured dog, so it's good camouflage, and would help me to creep up on rabbits or squirrel.

If I could find any!

AUTUMN

Autumn is foggy,

The ground gets all soggy,

My 'walkies' are always on mud.

There's rain, and more rain,

Then it just rains again,

'Til the rivers are swollen in flood.

The trees look so bare,

Their leaves are not there,

They've all fallen down to the ground.

I hunt for my prey,

But they've hidden away,

No squirrels are there to be found.

In front of my eyes,

It seems everything dies,

The flowers, the hedges, the trees.

No butterflies fly,

Their dance in the sky,

And there's no quiet hum from the bees.

But then I can see,

That beauty can be,

Any place, if you just use your eyes.

And I like how the ground,

Makes me hard to be found,

Autumn gives me the perfect disguise.

This poem is about one of the things I really love to eat as a treat!

Hu-Mum and Dog-Dad are very careful about what I eat. I always have good quality food. Chicken, steak, lamb, duck, liver, fish and fresh vegetables. Sometimes though we will eat out at a Dog Friendly pub or café, and lots of those have a Doggy Menu!

A menu!

Just for dogs!

How brilliant is that?

So, when we go to one of those places for lunch, I am always allowed my favourite thing from the Doggy Menu.

Sausages!!!!!

HOT DOG!

Sausages
Sausages
They're my favourite thing
Sausages
Sausages
Make me want to sing
Sausages
Sausages
This is what I wish
Sausages
Sausages
Filling up my dish

Brown and fat and juicy
Sizzling in the pan
I want to eat those Sausages
Any time I can

Sausages
Sausages
Meaty, tasty treat
Sausages
Sausages
The thing I want to eat
Sausages
Sausages
Jumbo ones or small
Sausages
Sausages
Are the best of all.

Except for steak!

This next poem is another one written by Hu-Mum about me!

I think it describes me very well. I don't want any of that ribbons and bows stuff, I'm too rough and tough for those!

Besides, I'd just lose them when I go hedgerow surfing anyway!

What's hedgerow surfing, you ask?

Diving into a hedge and squirming through looking for furry things.

It's fun!

Apart from the thorns and bits that stick to me!

WOOKIE

You may not be a show class dog,
You're scruffy, loud and bold,
You don't wear bows and ribbons,
Don't mind the snow and cold,
You love a muddy 'walkies',
You jump, and dig, and climb,
You roll in really stinky stuff,
You do it all the time.

You're not afraid of anything,
You're loyal, brave and true,
You'll go wherever we will go,
Do what we ask you too,
Despite you being tiny,
Your heart is supersize,
We see the beauty of your soul,
Shining in your eyes.

And you have so much love to give,
Although you're very small,
You might stand just ten inches,
But to us you're ten feet tall.

This poem I wrote in support of Betsy and Bronte.

Betsy and Bronte are also Yorkies, and they live with Hu-Mums friend, Angie.

They tell me Angie is a 'shopaholic', but not for herself….for them!

Okay, I 'may' have a 'couple' of coats and jumpers for the really, really horrible weather, but unlike most other dogs, we have hair, not fur, so we don't have a nice, dense undercoat to keep us warm and dry.

I would rather wear a coat or jumper than have to have a bath after EVERY walk.

Oh, for any of you NOT in the UK, The Range and B&M are shops that sell LOTS of dog clothes!

Betsy and Bronte

THE LAMENT OF BETSY AND BRONTE

We're not the sort to have a moan,

We're happy, cute and sweet,

But sometimes things just get too much,

We have to stamp our feet.

We have so many jumpers,

We just can't count them all,

Drawers, and drawers, and wardrobes full,

And hanging in the hall.

So, we're starting a petition,

A law to banish 'Them',

The bane of every Yorkies life,

The Range, and B&M.

When Hu-Mum goes out shopping,

We share a look of fear,

We know when she comes home again,

More jumpers will appear,

Dog-Dad says we've got enough,

He says we've got too many,

If we were given choices,

We'd rather not have any,

Or maybe one, or even two,

A girl must look her best,

So, maybe twenty jumpers each,

And throw away the rest.

Oh no – we're getting just as bad,

As Hu-Mum – that's a shock,

But at least it's only jumpers

We DO NOT WANT a frock!

This next poem is all about my favourite time of year.

I love the Spring.

Walkies at any time of year are wonderful, but there's just something about Spring.

Maybe it's because the daylight hours are getting longer, which means better and longer walkies. Perhaps it's because it's getting warmer, and all the rabbits and squirrels are coming out after hiding for most of the winter.

Things to chase again!

SPRING

Spring has sprung,

It's just begun,

It is my favourite season.

I must get out,

And run about,

And bark for no good reason.

New flowers grow,

Warm breezes blow,

And fresh leaves deck the trees.

The birds all sing,

Upon the wing,

To join the hum of bees.

The rabbits run,

Beneath the sun,

The squirrels leap and climb.

With every dawn,

New life is born,

Spring really is sublime.

This is the first poem written by one of my friends, although she wasn't my friend at the start.

Pixie is the old lady of our furry family.

She's a big cat, bigger than me, and she wasn't too pleased when I first arrived.

That was my fault as the first thing I did was yap at her, jump around like a lunatic, and then steal her ball and run off with it.

I know…..but I WAS very young.

I have better manners now, and even though I might have deserved a slap from her sometimes, she never did.

PIXIE

PAWSOME POOCH

I never had much time for dogs, I find them loud and rude,

All bark, and drool, and slobbery jaws, and bolting down their food,

They scratch, and smell, and misbehave, no manners shown at all,

I used to think their only skill was peeing up a wall.

So, when that puppy first arrived, I wasn't pleased at all,

Especially when it yapped at me, then stole my jingly ball,

It wanted me to play with it, I wasn't having that,

A pup was not acceptable, to such a genteel cat.

But then that feral cat came round, and caught me by surprise,

I couldn't run, I couldn't hide, my life flashed past my eyes,

It pinned me by the garden fence, I thought my life was done,

But someone heard my cries for help, and came at flat-out run.

She charged straight up the garden path, she was an awesome sight,

Barking like a Hound from Hell she gave that cat a fright,

It ran off like a total wimp, from a pup just three months old,

And now that dog is my best friend, the bravest of the bold.

This poem is about squirrels.

I might have already mentioned squirrels once or twice, but they really are ANNOYING!

They run in front of me just fast enough so I can't catch them, and then they run up a tree!

I'm sure that's cheating!

Then, to make things worse, they sit on a branch above my head and say rude things in squirrel language.

However, I've been practising and practising, and the next time that sneaky squirrel will get a nasty shock!

Ta-dah!!!!

Can you spot me?

SNEAKY SQUIRRELS

I love to chase the squirrels

I notice in the park,

I try to creep up quietly,

And never even bark,

But every time they see me,

And get up off the ground,

I'm left below, frustrated,

Just circling round and round,

They sit up in the branches,

And tease me from on high,

It really is the only time,

I wish that I could fly,

I'd take off like an eagle

And fly up at top speed,

And catch those squirrels napping,

That would be good indeed,

But though I am so many things,

An eagle I am not,

So, I have had to think quite hard,

To plan, and scheme, and plot,

And now I have the answer,

The truth is plain to see,

To catch that sneaky squirrel,

I must become the tree.

This next poem is all about my lovely Dog-Dad.

EVERY week day he takes me for awesome walkies while Hu-Mum is at work, and we go to different woods and fields so I don't get bored.

He never forgets to carry water for me, which I need because I do LOTS of running.

He takes us away for brilliant holidays too.

Especially to Wales.

I love Wales!

DOG-DAD

There's lots of other Dog-Dads

But you're the best of all,

You never tire of throwing,

My frisbee, or my ball,

You take me for great 'walkies',

You let me have my fun,

You point out sneaky squirrels,

And watch me make them run,

We walk for lots of miles,

We amble far and wide,

You let me check the hedgerows,

And squirm my way inside,

You let me have a paddle,

And climb a fallen tree,

You give me time to sniff and search,

You let me just be 'me',

You don't care if I'm muddy,

You don't care if I'm wet,

You really are the greatest Dad,

A dog could ever get.

This poem is another one written by one of my friends, Clementine Wonky-Beak.

One day, Hu-Mum told me that she was getting some chickens.

I like chicken, so I was happy.

But Hu-Mum meant LIVE chickens!

She had heard of a Rescue that saved ex-commercial hens from slaughter at just 72 weeks old.

These chickens had never lived outside, just in cages in a big barn.

I thought that was sad.

So, five chickens came to live in our garden. They arrived looking ready to go straight into the oven, but they soon looked really lovely.

Sadly, Clementine Wonky-Beak flew over the Rainbow Bridge last year, as lots of ex-commercials don't live a long time, but at least she died free, and with a name.

CLEMENTINE WONKY-BEAK

A FRESH START

I used to live in a great big barn,
With thousands just like me,
No room to move, no space to breathe,
The lights on constantly.
I never looked up at the sky,
Or knew the night from day,
My life was there within those walls,
To lay, and lay, and lay.
I never knew the touch of rain,
The warmth of summer sun,
The joy of having freedom,
To dust bathe, scratch and run.

I lived there in that great big barn,
With thousands just the same,
And I was just a number,
I didn't have a name.
I didn't have a future,
My time was running out,
Produce, produce, produce or die,
That's what it's all about.
But someone came to that great big barn,
For the thousands and for me,
And now my life is wonderful,
I'm loved, and I am free.

This poem is about another Yorkie.

Ralphie lives with Catherine, another one of Hu-Mums friends.

He's a bit............................. odd!

Actually, he's REALLY odd, but Catherine loves him anyway. Very lovable, us Yorkies!

RALPHIE

RALPHIE

I have a friend called Ralphie,

He's just a little strange,

He has a set of crazy rules,

That he will never change.

The street is his dominion,

The postie he would banish,

And as for parcel companies,

He wishes they would vanish.

If you want his attention,

You'd better offer food,

Of he will look right through you,

And stomp off in a mood.

He wants to be Head Honcho,

He doesn't want to share,

He wants the lap, he wants the bed,

The sofa AND the chair.

No groomers, vets or visitors,

No TV after 10,

And if you need to go for walks,

Then HE will tell you when.

He will not take his tablets,

Not even wrapped in cheese,

And as for baths or showers,

Well………..he'd rather live with fleas.

Do you remember how earlier I mentioned I was very brave with some sheep?

It happened when I was only quite young.

We had gone to Wales, and were exploring a Country Park, and then there were these sheep. They shouldn't have been there, but the naughty things had broken through a fence.

I really thought they were going to eat Hu-Mum and Dog-Dad so I had to protect them.

Of course, I've seen millions of sheep since then, and now I know they don't eat people. So, I don't scare them, and they don't scare me.

Seems fair!

FEELING SHEEPISH

I always have to stay at heel by horses, cows and sheep,
I'm not allowed to chase them, or make them run and leap,
Hu-Mum says they are taboo, I mustn't cause them harm,
So, I am always very good when walking by a farm.

But once in Wales we met some sheep, who'd broken out to stray,
We turned a corner of the path and they were in the way,
We all stopped, we all stood, and no-one made a move,
I didn't even make a sound, Hu-Mum would not approve.

One sheep then took another step and I had to move too,
I must protect my Humans, it's just what dogs will do.
I jumped in front of Hu-Mum and gave that sheep 'The Stare',
The look that says 'Just try it. Come closer if you dare!'.

That sheep was really massive. I was smaller than its head,
But I'm a proper Yorkie so I wasn't filled with dread,
I stood my ground, I stared it down, I wasn't going to run,
I bared my teeth to show that sheep my fight had just begun.

We stood there for long moments, the time was ticking by,
That sheep and I like statues, just staring eye to eye,
And then they all just turned away, they didn't want to fight,
And we could finish off our walk with no more sheep in sight.

This poem is all about where dogs come from.

I don't mean nowadays; I mean WAY back.

Right at the start.

We are all descended from wolves.

We all still have many of their instincts and genetic memory.

No-one ever told me that eating grass if I have a funny tummy will make me feel better.

I just KNOW.

No-one ever taught me how to hunt.

I just KNOW.

That's the wolf within!

THE WOLF WITHIN

Way back in the distant past,

A wolf first walked with Man,

And from that small beginning,

A partnership began.

Down through the millennia,

The wolfs appearance changed,

Mankind transformed it, for their needs

Its body rearranged

And they have been there ever since,

Walking by Mans side,

Guard, protector, hunter, friend,

Companion and guide.

Loyal, brave and gentle,

But fierce if there's a need,

They can be so many things,

And follow where you lead.

And though breeds now are so diverse,

The long, the short, the tall,

The wolf still lives inside of us,

The father of us all.

This next poem is actually a commission!

For Ralphie.

Remember Ralphie?

Well, he has to share his home with another dog, and he really isn't happy about it.

She bullies him!

I think he's maybe just a bit of a big baby, but this is the poem I wrote for him after he told me all about Peggy Sue.

I'm sure she isn't really THAT bad, but the poem made Ralphie happy.

I just hope Peggy Sue never sees it!

PEGGY SUE

PEGGY SUE

There is a certain Devil Dog,

Her name is Peggy Sue,

She looks so sweet and lovable,

But that is just not true!

She bullies poor old Ralphie,

She really makes him squeak,

And not just sometimes, now and then,

But every day, each week.

She's not the brightest either,

She hasn't got a clue,

She just spins round in circles,

When she's not sure what to do.

And then she'll hide beneath a chair,

And lurk there in the dark,

Until she launches an attack,

Just like a Great White shark.

I'm sure a really sweet dog lies,

Somewhere – beneath that fur,

But I'm not willing to find out,

I'll stay away from her.

This is another poem not written by me.

It's by the chickens.

Mercedes, Daffodil, Eleanor, Grizabella and Houdini.

The cats are nervous of the chickens, but I get on very well with them

And, of course, I sort out any rats that come into the garden to try to steal their food.

WHO'S CHICKEN?

We are the garden Mafia,

We rule each inch of ground,

We terrorise the neighbours' cats,

If they try to come round.

We eat it if it's edible,

And sometimes if it's not,

We hunt out every bug and snail,

And then we scoff the lot.

We tolerate no trespassers,

Not even family cats,

We chase away all other birds,

But worst of all are rats.

It's said no matter where you are,

A rat is somewhere near,

They'll steal your food, quite brazenly,

They really have no fear.

We try our best to peck them,

But they're clever and they're fast,

You see them there, and then you blink,

And then they have run past.

But we do have an ally,

Who's fighting for our cause,

That tiny, little hairy dog,

Is DEATH on four small paws!

This poem is all about how we communicate.

Some people call us 'Dumb Animals', because we can't talk.

Of course we can talk, but I don't mean with sounds!

Our eyes, our ears, our tails, our whole bodies 'speak' to you.

We CAN talk, you just need to learn how to 'listen'.

NOT SO DUMB

I wish I could talk,
Say 'Let's take a walk',
Or 'May I have lamb steak for tea'.
Or debate whether ball,
Is the best toy of all,
Or discuss how I love running free.
We could chat about cats,
Or chasing the rats,
And rabbits and squirrels and deer,
We could moan about rain,
Till the sun's out again,
And the weather is perfect and clear.
We could laugh at the storm,
When we're safe in the warm,
And I'm happy sat there on your lap.
And last thing at night,
I would whisper 'Sleep tight'
Then settle on down for a nap.

I wish I could say,
That every day,
My life is just perfect with you.
But sadly, I'm dumb,
The words will not come,
So, this poem will just have to do.

This poem is about toys.

I love toys.

Balls are my favourite, but I also love playing tug of war with Hu-Mum, and anything that squeaks!

Every now and then, Hu-Mum decides I have too many toys!

Too many?

How can there ever be too many?

Then she sorts out ones I don't really play with, and gives them to the local Dog Rescue, for the poor dogs who don't have humans of their own.

I don't mind that.

ALL dogs should have toys.

TOY STORY

I'm feeling quite hard done by,

No new toys for a week,

Dog-Dad says I've got enough,

But some of them DON'T SQUEAK!

I've got a massive toy box,

It's filled right up with stuff,

But I'm an active Yorkie,

It doesn't seem enough,

So I will have to forage,

For something I've forgot,

But digging down is difficult,

I do have quite a lot,

Toys that jingle, toys that squeak

Toys that bounce and spin,

I've only rummaged halfway down

And almost fallen in,

I'm worried I'll get buried,

Be stuck in there all day,

So maybe I'll just stick with ball,

My favourite thing to play.

This poem is about the gerbils! Which ARE NOT RATS!

Dog-Dad was amused by the way I was so obsessed by the Hamsters, Guinea Pigs and Gerbils in the local pet store, so thought it would be fun to get some for me to watch at home.

So that's how we ended up with Vader and Yoda. YES…..that Star Wars thing again.

If I could roll my eyes, I would! They do keep me and Solo entertained, though!

GERBILS ARE NOT RATS

Gerbils are not rats,

I'm told that is a fact,

And though I'd like to bite them,

They have to stay intact.

Gerbils are not rats,

They must be left alone,

I'm not allowed to grab them,

And crunch through to the bone.

Gerbils are not rats,

They're not a tasty snack,

I'm just allowed to look at them,

And not launch an attack.

Gerbils are not rats,

I find it quite confusing,

They certainly resemble rats,

It really is bemusing.

This is a poem about Summer.

I know some humans really like the very hot weather, and lie out in the sun trying to get a tan, but for us dogs it's really not very nice when it's too warm.

It can be dangerous for us, too.

Luckily Hu-Mum and Dog-Dad know this, and when it's very, very hot they either invent games for me to play inside, or find somewhere safe to go!

Like the river!

I love paddling in the water!

SUMMER

I like a lovely, sunny day,
It's better than the rain,
But when the summer gets too hot,
It really is a pain.

I can't walk on the pavement,
Because it burns my feet,
And it's not safe to run around,
I just don't like the heat.

We get up really early,
To take a walk outside,
But when the sun is blazing down,
I stay inside and hide.

Too hot to run, too hot to walk,
Too hot to even sit,
I do not like these temperatures,
Not even just a bit.

But now we have the answer,
We go down to the stream,
And in the shade beneath the trees,
It really is a dream.

I splash, and swim, and cool right down,
Protected from the sun,
I don't mind summer days like these,
They really are such fun.

This poem is about Hu-Mums Mum.

She tells me to call her Grandma.

Grandma is more of a cat person. She has lots!

More than THREE!

She always calls me Stink Dog, but I know she loves me really.

That's because I am always such a 'Good Girl'.

I behave beautifully when we meet up for a meal.

I would NEVER steal food!

GRANDMA

Grandma likes to wind me up,

She does it really well,

She always calls me 'Stink Dog',

Although I DO NOT SMELL.

She says that cats are better,

And dogs are misbegotten,

But then she gives me cuddles,

And really spoils me rotten.

She says that I'm so well behaved,

I'm never loud or rude,

She loves how when we're out for lunch,

I never beg for food,

I settle down so patiently,

Just sitting by a chair,

I never make a single sound,

You wouldn't know I'm there.

She shows me off to everyone,

She tells them I'm so good,

You'd even think that I was hers,

Until you understood.

So, though she might deny it,

I see her full of pride,

And know she loves me really,

That cannot be denied!

This poem is written by my feline friend, Solo.

I knew she would give me trouble about it!

She moaned so much you'd think I'd asked her to jump into a bath!

I would never do that, she's a real baby when it comes to getting wet!

All I asked for was ONE poem.

She moaned about it for days, and then did it anyway!

Cats are SO contrary!

STUPID POEM

Wookie told me, 'Write a poem'

I said 'What? But I'm a cat,

We don't do what we are told to,

We're free spirits, not a dog,

Sitting on a stupid log.

So no, I'm never, ever doing that'

But she sat and gave me 'sad eyes',

What's a cat supposed to do?

So, I wrote this stupid poem,

And I even made it rhyme,

Well, at least, some of the time,

Seems I'm pretty good at poems too.

But I still think that poetry's stupid,

I can't be bothered, it's a chore,

So, this is my final verse,

I'm off outside,

To try to hide,

I'm not prepared to write down any more!

This poem is about when Hu-Mum and Dog-Dad helped another cat and her kittens.

They had lost their home, and so they came to stay with us.

The Mum cat was called Eevee, named after a Pokémon, whatever one of those is!

Hu-Mum said it was silly to name a cat after a fictional creature.

Pixie, Solo, Vader, Yoda and I just looked at each other!

The kittens have now gone to fabulous Forever homes, but Eevee is staying with us.

NEW FAMILY

My Humans love all animals,

They're very, very kind,

They're always ready to help out,

If one is in a bind,

So, when they got a cry for help,

They acted straight away,

And that's how little Eevee

And her kittens came to stay.

A Mum cat and her babies,

Were really in great need,

They'd lost their home, poor little things,

So very sad indeed,

And so, they came to stay with us,

I didn't mind at all,

Kittens are great fun to watch,

When they are very small.

I loved to watch them playing,

And running all around,

I was so sad when they grew up,

And then new homes were found,

But Eevee's going nowhere,

She's staying here with us,

As Hu-Mum said 'It's just one more,

It's really no great fuss!'.

is another poem that Hu-Mum wrote about me.

It's obvious that Hu-Mum loves me very much, and she doesn't care if I get muddy, and look scruffy.

She says 'Be a dog, Wookie. Just be a dog.'

So, I 'just dog.'

I'm not always mucky and scruffy though.

Sometimes I can look clean, and neat and tidy.

For maybe five minutes!

WOOKIE

There are so many Yorkies,

But you're the one for me,

Whether on my lap for cuddles,

Or climbing up a tree,

Or scaring all the squirrels,

Or chasing after ball,

Or getting really filthy,

When into mud you fall.

Your energy is boundless,

You'll walk for miles each day,

And then as soon as we get home,

Pick up a toy to play,

You're tireless and relentless,

You don't know how to quit,

And nothing ever fazes you,

Not even just a bit.

You're brave, and true, and loyal,

I've loved you from the start,

Yes, I may be your owner,

But you sure own my heart.

This is a poem about walkies.

Walkies are THE BEST!

My favourite walkies are in woods and forests, and we are lucky to have some close to our home, but we will also travel to ones further away at weekends, and much further away on holidays.

I NEVER forget anywhere I've been to before. I get excited even before we've finally arrived.

Hu-Mum says I must have something like a Google Pin in my brain and it starts 'pinging' when we get close!

Woods are just awesome!

Wyre Forest.

WALKIES!

I love to go for walkies,

It's what I live to do,

I have my favourite places,

But I do like somewhere new.

Some walkies are quite close to home,

But some are really far,

I always get excited,

When we go out in the car.

And when we drive for ages,

We're going somewhere great,

A place for special walkies,

I really just can't wait.

Now, some dogs love the beaches,

But they're not to my taste,

All that space, but with no trees,

It just seems like a waste.

The woods are where I want to be,

They're where I really thrive,

The sounds, the smells, the chance to chase,

That's where I feel alive.

And when we find a great new place,

I'll log it in my brain,

Just like a canine Google Pin,

Until we go again.

So next time I'll remember,

Exactly where we are,

And I'll be all excited,

To get out of the car.

This is a poem by the Gerbils (ARE NOT RATS!)

I don't know whether it was Yoda or Vader who wrote it, or maybe they wrote it together.

I have listened to Hu-Mum about NOT eating the gerbils, but the cats still haven't given up.

They can't get to them though.

Stupid cats!

YODA AND VADER.

GERBIL POWER

My bro and me are Gerbils,

We live life in our cage,

We like to wind the felines up,

And put them in a rage.

Those cats go really frantic,

They think we're good to eat,

But if they put their paws too close,

We bite them on their feet.

We know that they can't get us,

We sit there feeling smug,

And call them nasty nicknames,

Like 'Useless, hairy rug'.

They stare at us with venom,

They'd love to make us scream,

But they are not allowed to,

It's just a futile dream.

This poem is about Winter.

Lots of dogs and humans don't like the winter, but I really don't mind.

I love snow!

Snow is awesome!

Much better than rain, rain, rain.

When it's REALLY cold, all the mud freezes too, so I don't get filthy and need a bath after walkies!

Bonus!

WINTER

I love a bright, crisp winter day,
With drifts of fresh laid snow,
While other dogs just stay at home,
I must get out and go.
I love the crunch with every step,
The cold and clean fresh air,
I love to follow animal tracks,
Meandering here and there.

I love the way the world has changed,
Familiar now seems new,
I like the way that in the shade,
The snow looks almost blue.
I love the way that branches hang,
All laden in the hedge,
I love the ice that creaks and groans,
Along the duck pond edge.

I love how snow drops from the trees,
A gentle, drifting rain,
I love the snowflakes silent fall,
To coat the trees again,
I love the frozen stillness,
Of grass, and hedge and tree,
Winter has its beauty,
You just need eyes to see.

I've mentioned before about being able to go with Hu-Mum and Dog-Dad to places where we can get a meal.

Of course, we have our favourite ones, and there is one in a village not far away where I always get THE best welcome.

The Long Itchington Diner.

The ladies in there LOVE me.

They call me 'The Diner Mascot', and I know that if Hu-Mum and Dog-Dad were ever abducted by aliens, I could go and live there and be The Diner Dog!

Not that I WANT Hu-Mum and Dog-Dad to be abducted, obviously, but it's nice to have an option!

DINER DOG

When we go for walkies,

It's nice to take a break,

Where I can have a sausage,

And Dog-Dad have some cake,

Lots of cafes in our parks,

Say dogs are welcome too,

So, stopping for a little rest,

Seems like the thing to do.

Sometimes we find a country pub,

Where we can have a meal,

Then carry on with walkies,

That really is ideal,

Or sometimes we'll have breakfast first,

Then carry on all day,

I don't mind it that way round,

I'm happy either way.

Some places are dog tolerant,

We have to stay outside,

But some are so dog friendly,

We're welcomed right inside.

Of course, we have our favourites,

The ones we use a lot,

And when we turn up at one place,

I'm in there like a shot.

The lovely Long Itch Diner,

Is my favourite place to be,

The way the ladies welcome me,

I feel like Royalty!

This next poem is about Wales.

I first went to Wales when I was only five months old. I've loved it ever since.

It has so many lovely places to walk, and to stay for a holiday.

Forests and mountains to walk for miles and miles.

My favourite place to stay has its own river, an acre of meadow, and is just a bit different!

CYMRU CANINE

There is a place I like to go,
I've loved since I was young,
A place that is so wonderful,
Its beauty has been sung.

A land of misty mountains,
Of snow-scent on the breeze,
A land that tells of olden times,
Amongst its ancient trees.

A land of ruined castles,
A land that tells of strife,
A land where people battled,
To save their way of life.

A land of myth and magic,
Where legends are still told,
The tales of one Red Dragon,
Who lived there, fierce and bold.

A place that gets into your heart,
That wipes your cares away,
A place that soothes your very soul,
A place that bids you – Stay!

This is my final poem.

It's about a time of year that millions of Humans look forward to, especially the tiny ones!

Christmas.

The children get so excited, making wishes about what they would like to get.

So, I thought I would make a wish too!

MY CHRISTMAS WISH

If I could make a Christmas wish,

I know what it would be,

It wouldn't be for juicy bones.

Or toys beneath the tree,

It wouldn't be for a nice new ball,

Or a snuggly, comfy bed,

It wouldn't be for me at all,

This is my wish instead.

I wish that every Rescue dog,

Could find a loving home,

Where they will be so wanted,

And no longer be alone,

I wish for them the loving arms,

To cuddle them so tight,

The gentle hands, the gentle voice,

That tells them 'It's alright!'.

I wish for them long walkies,

And days spent in the sun,

And no more being hungry,

Or afraid of everyone,

I wish for them the freedom,

To run, and jump, and play,

I wish for them the joy I feel,

Each and every day.

I wish for them true happiness,

An end to pain and fear,

I wish for them a family,

That is my wish this year.

That's it.

That is the end of my poems……..for now.

I hope you have enjoyed reading them, and maybe they will inspire YOUR dog to try their paw at poetry.

Now I'm going to have a rest, and then head off to the woods to chase squirrels.

Woofs, wags and licks,

Wookie.

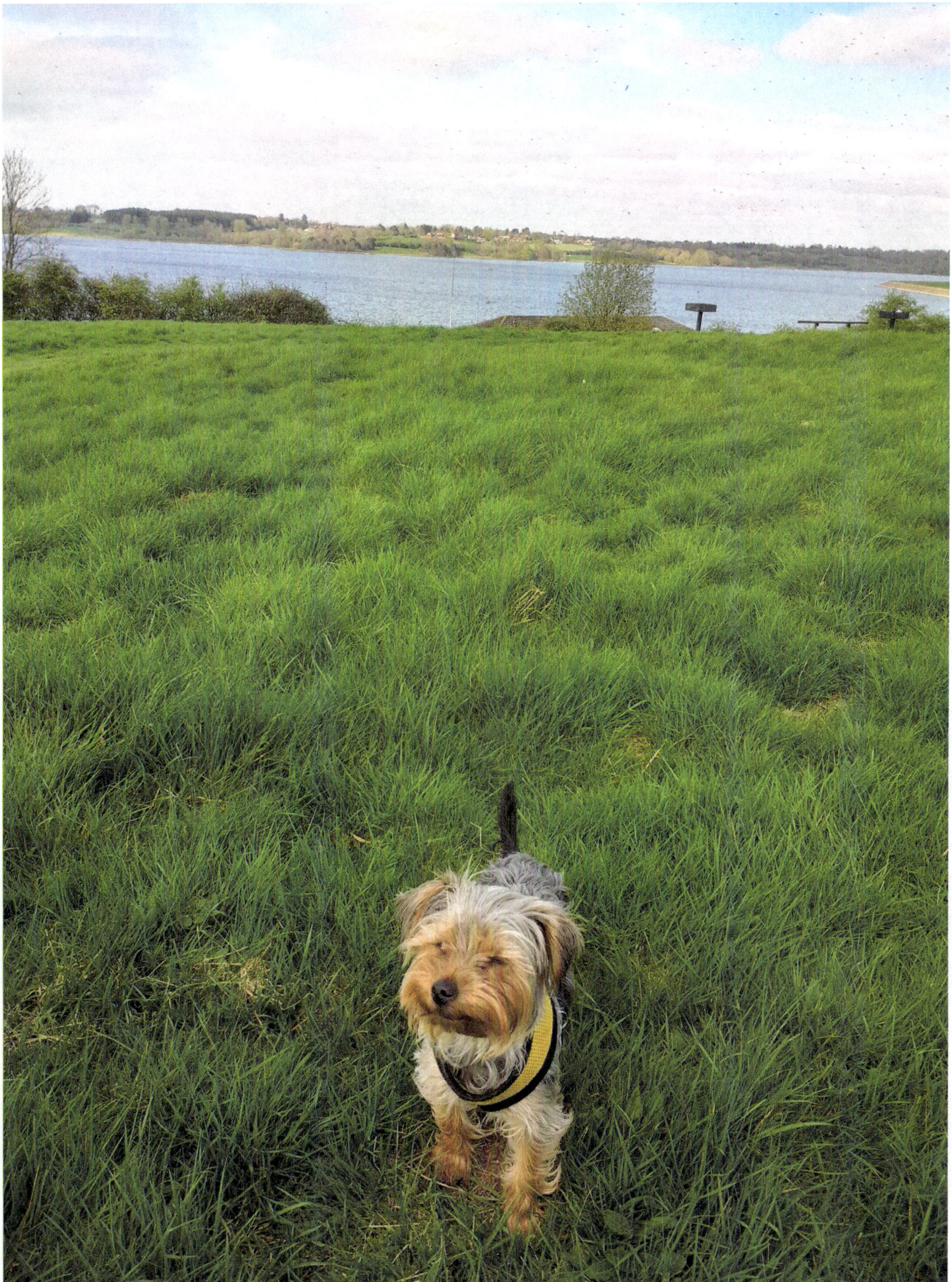

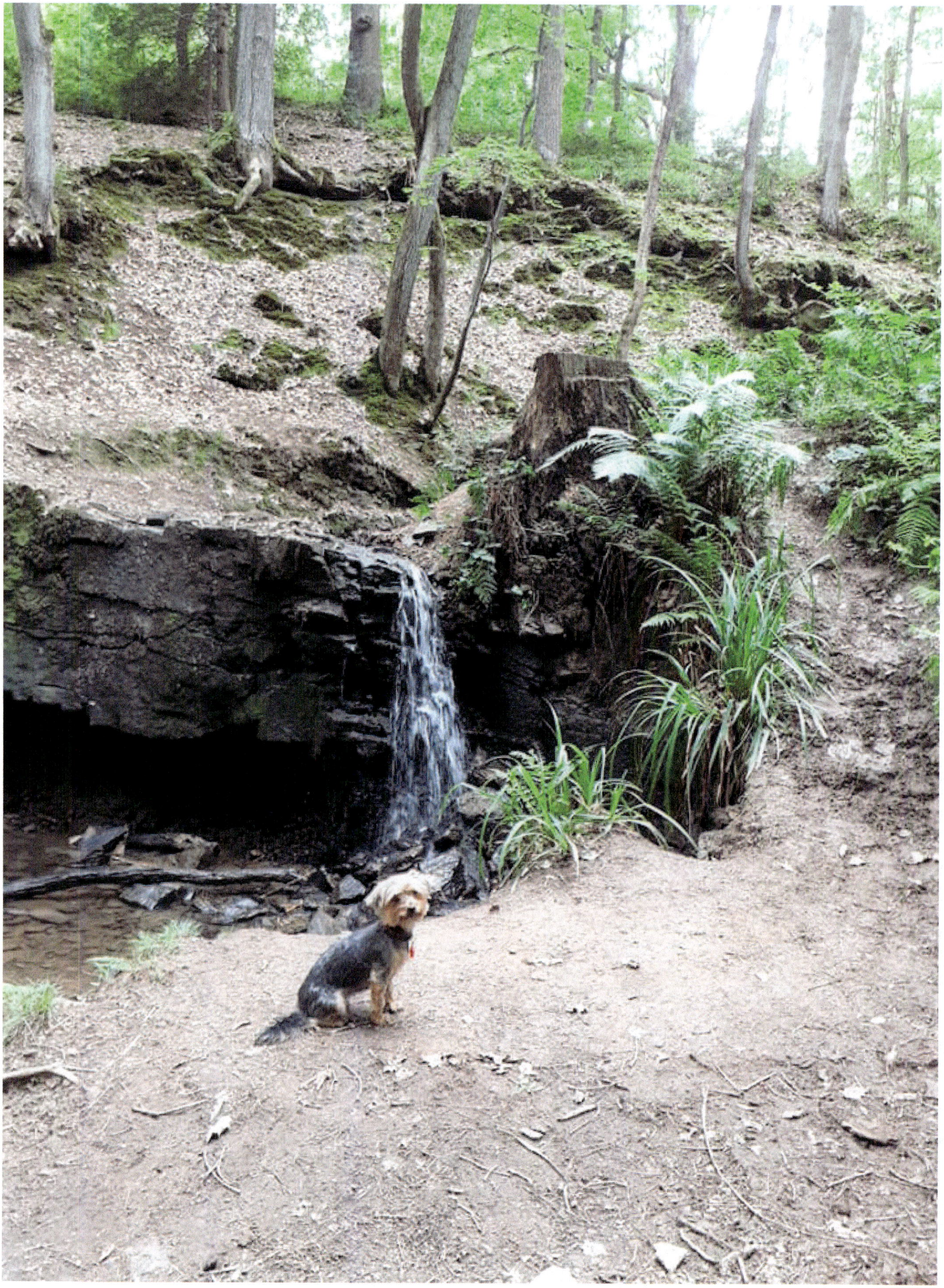

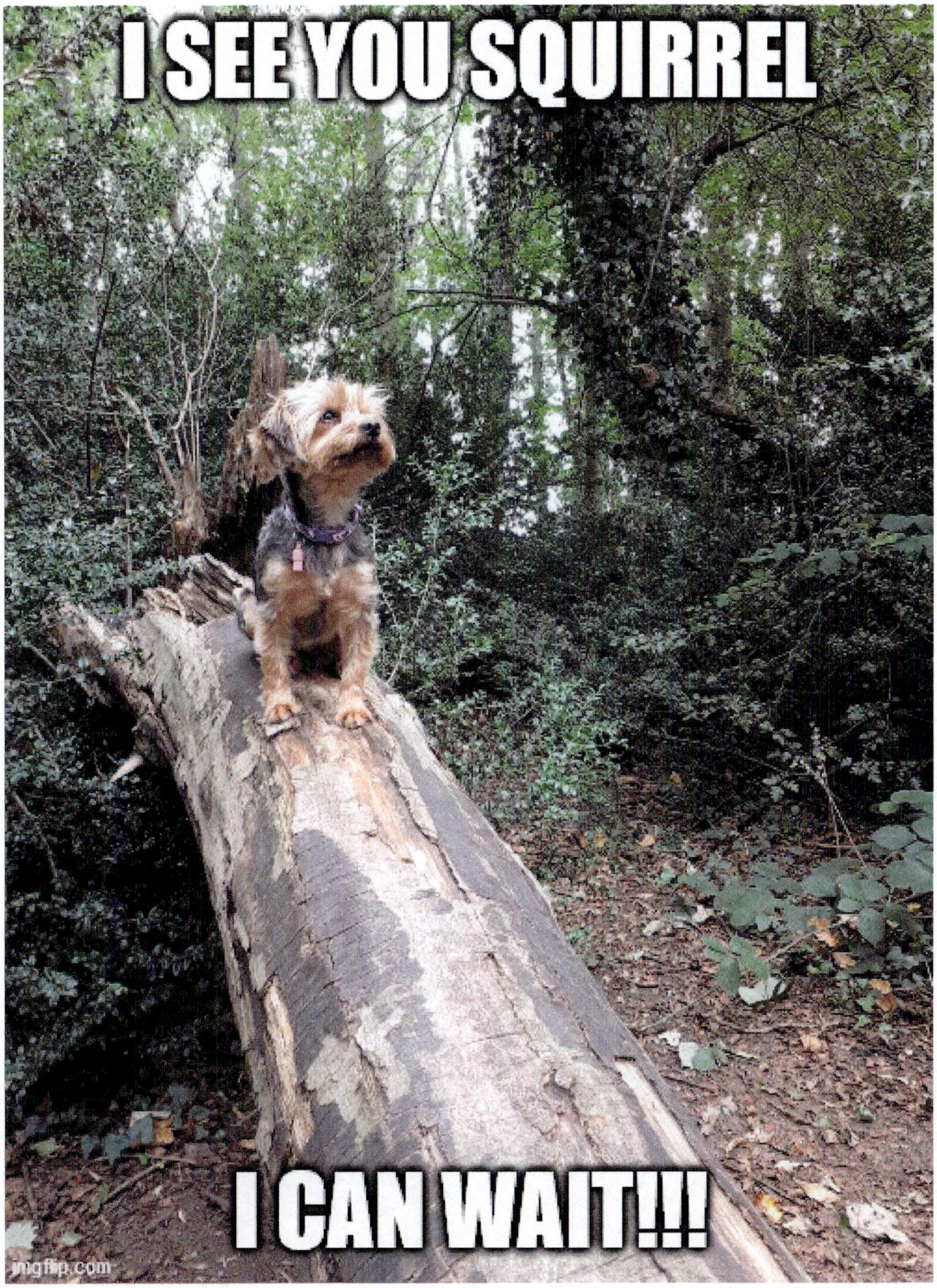
I SEE YOU SQUIRREL
I CAN WAIT!!!
imgflip.com

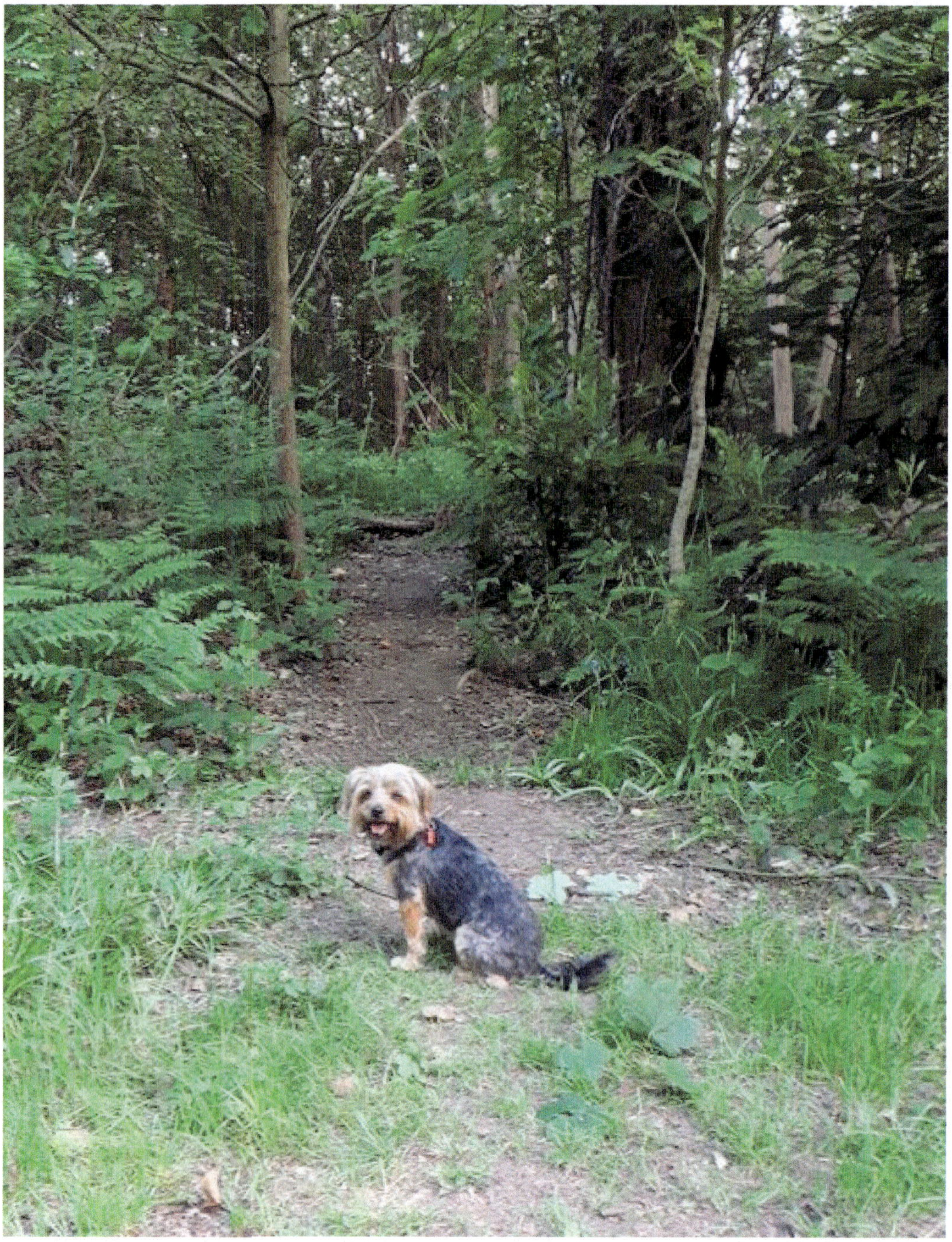

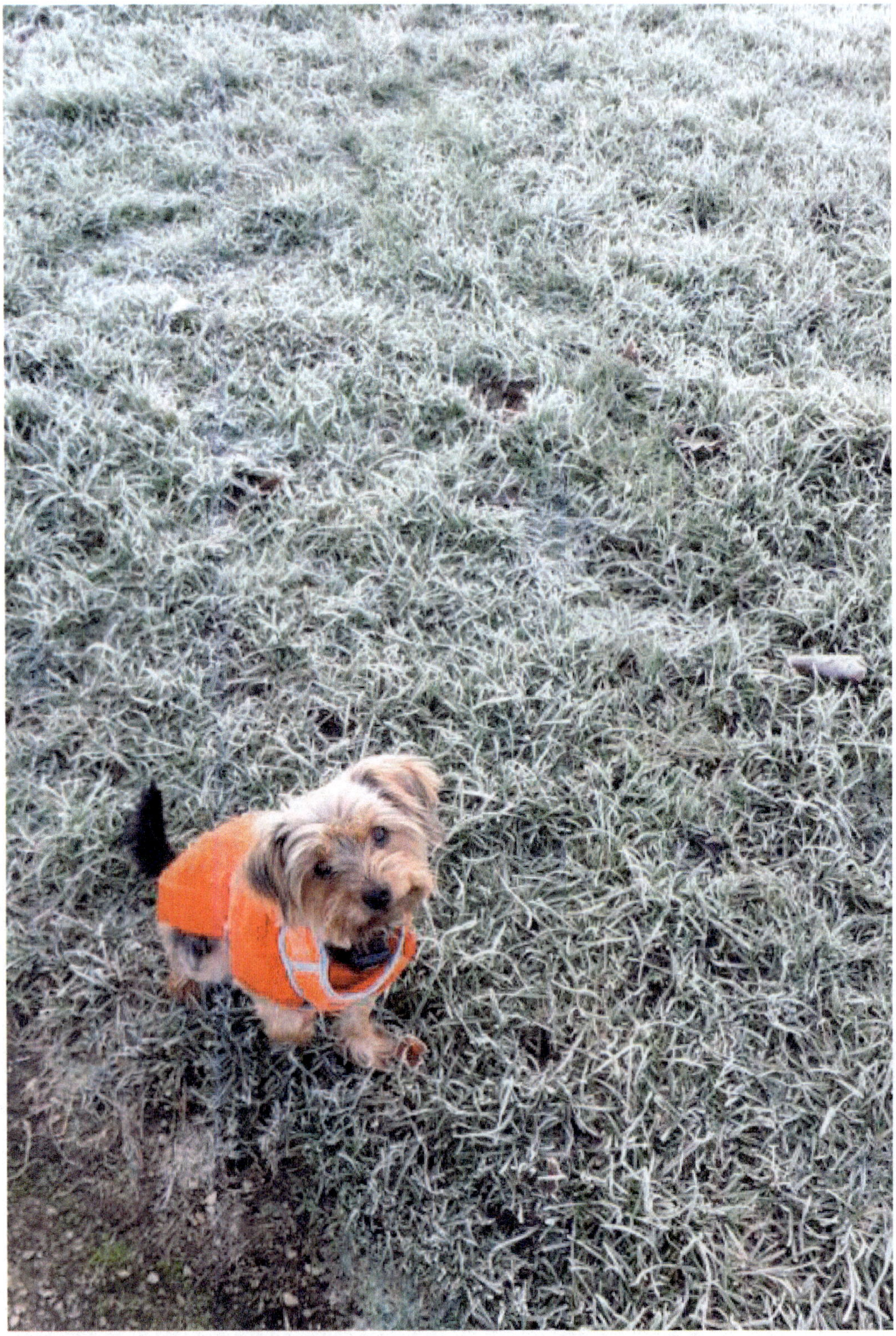

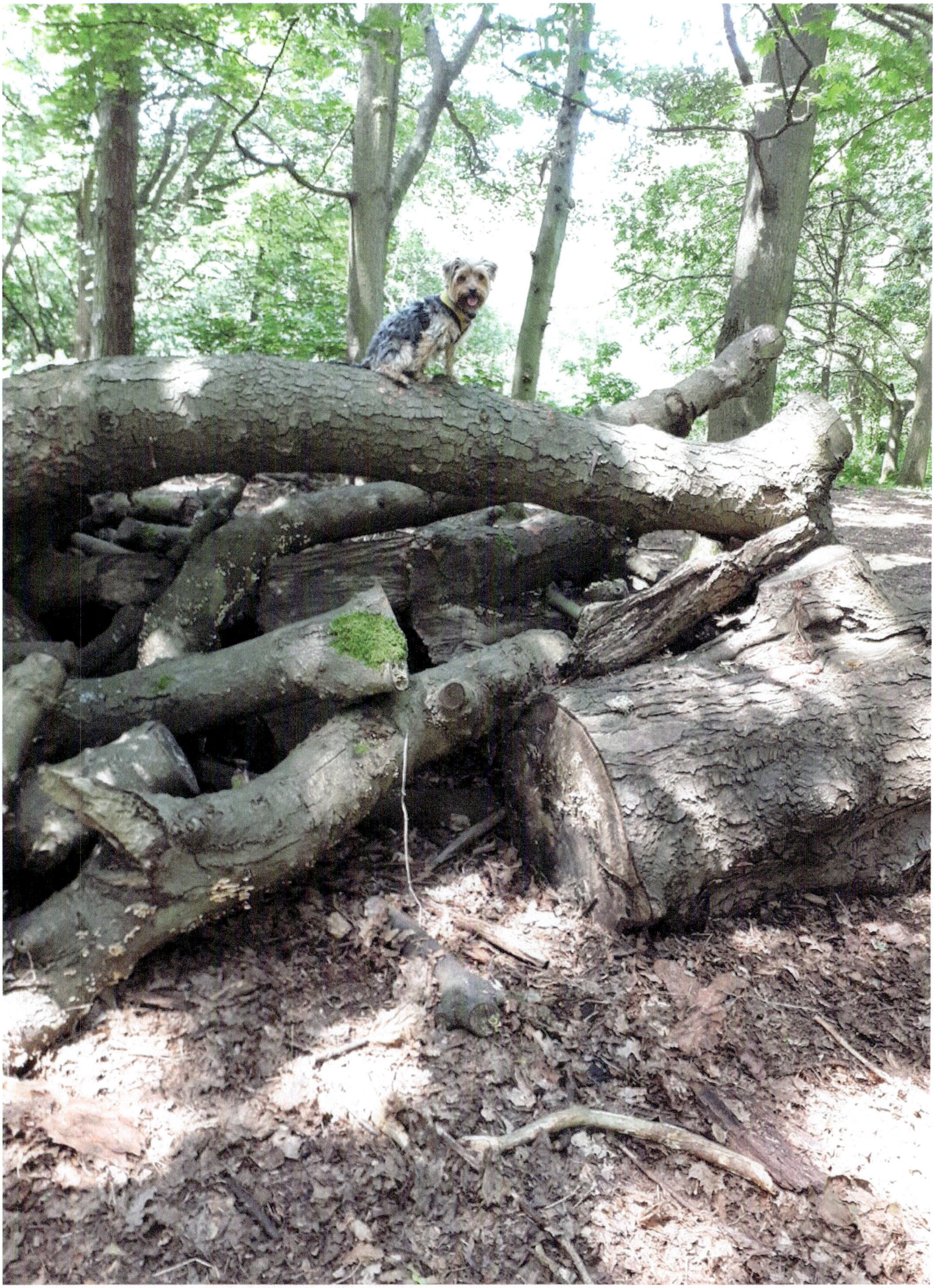

Printed in Great Britain
by Amazon